Can Your Dog Do Your Homework?:
And Other Questions about Animals

by Ms. Hess's class
with Tony Stead

capstone

Dogs on Computers

by Kindi

Can my dog do my homework? What? That's just not possible.

I use my hands to type and move a mouse. My dog uses its paws to walk and run.

I guess I won't ask my dog to type my book report.

IS this Good?

Whimpering Wolves

by Jackson

Can a wolf make a phone call? No, that's not possible.

People use their words and make sentences. Wolves communicate by howling, whimpering, growling, and barking.

I guess I don't need to let a wolf use my new smart phone.

Hello?
Howl

Feeding Frenzy

by Madilynn

Do bats have fingers? They do, but not like ours.

They use their bodies to get bugs. Here's how they do it. They swing their wings and catch the bug with their tail. Then they put the bug in their mouth.

People eat with forks and spoons. But a bat uses its body. I guess a bat doesn't need silverware.

second finger
third finger
thumb
wing membrane
fifth finger
fourth finger
tail

Amazing Fish

by Garrett

Do fish go to school like people? No, that isn't possible. I go to school, so I can learn to read and write.

A school of fish is different from a school for people. Fish travel in a school, so they can stay together and be safe.

A fish wouldn't learn a lot at our school.

School
of fish

Playful Cats

by Elizabeth

Can my cat play football? No! That's impossible!

I use my hands to throw and catch. A cat uses its paws to run, jump, walk, and play.

My cat can't play football, so I will play by myself.

POP!

Penguin Parents

by Oliver and Sawyer

Can a penguin take care of a human baby? No way! That couldn't happen.

A human mother feeds her baby milk and wraps the baby in a blanket. A penguin feeds its young with food it chews.

It wouldn't be a good idea to have a penguin as a babysitter.

Big, Strong Ants

by Dillon

Could you carry something much bigger than you? No, that would be very hard to do.

Ants can carry 50 times their weight. They have muscles inside their bodies. They also have mouth parts they can use to hold the leaf they are carrying.

I'm glad I don't have to carry heavy things all the way home like an ant does.

Animals are unique! A dog cannot do your homework, but it does many other important things.

What are some special things you've seen animals do?